# Gann Secrets Revealed

*Volume I:*
*Beyond Symbolism*
*in*
*Financial Astrology*

*by*

# TIM BOST

Harmonic Research Associates
Sarasota, Florida, USA

Gann Secrets Revealed: Beyond Symbolism in Financial Astrology

Copyright © 2001, 2003, 2009 Timothy L. Bost

All rights reserved under all Copyright Conventions.

*Submit all requests for reprinting to:*
Harmonic Research Associates
Post Office Box 1657
Sarasota, Florida 34230-1657 USA

Published in the United States of America by Harmonic Research Associates.

www.HarmonicResearchAssociates.com

Portions previously published as "Beyond Symbolism in Financial Astrology" & "Astro-Money Report #3" by Taylor-Bost in Sarasota, Florida, USA

Revised & Expanded Edition

ISBN-10: 1-933198-13-3
ISBN-13: 978-1-933198-13-2

EAN: 9781933198132

# GANN SECRETS REVEALED

*Volume I:*

*Beyond Symbolism in Financial Astrology*

**GANN SECRETS REVEALED**

# TABLE OF CONTENTS

# INTRODUCTION TO THE REVISED EDITION

Early in 2001, I was working with one of my private clients who told me he was looking for ways to sharpen up his approach to trading so that he could take money out of the markets more consistently. I had traveled to spend several days with him in his office, and as we sat at his conference table for one of our extended coaching sessions, our conversation turned from an examination of specific timing questions to a discussion of the price levels in trading situations. We had shared the observation that prices will often seemed to get pulled back to certain levels, or will try in vain to move past particular levels, during the progress of trading for a stock or a futures contract.

"There's sometimes more going on that meets the eye," I said. "In many cases stock prices are directly linked to specific planetary positions."

"Oh?" my client said. "Tell me more." While he certainly wasn't new to astrology—I was, after all, there to help him improve his skills as an astro-trader—this particular concept was new to him, and he was clearly excited about the implications that it had for his trading.

And so it was that for the next couple of hours I did my best to explain the basic connections between prices and zodiacal positions, and how they function in the markets, based on what I had learned from studying the work of W. D. Gann. Our discussion became quite animated, and by the end of our conversation that day I had a pile of sheets from a yellow legal pad scribbled with the notes and drawings that I had made in my effort to explain vibratory resonance and power numbers.

Those notes soon became the basis for a brief article and then, for the first edition of a monograph titled *Beyond Symbolism in Financial Astrology*.

This little book, published in 2003 as "Astro-Money Report #3" in a series of monographs that included the original editions of *J.P. Morgan's Billion-Dollar Secret* and *How to Find the Money in Your Horoscope,* became one of my most widely circulated publications.

I think because it took a simple, direct approach, many individuals got involved with this book and profited from it—and they let me know about their experiences. I got letters and emails from people who had read it, when I lectured at conferences and workshops I often got questions that either referred to the material in the book or dealt with matters that had been addressed in its pages.

That confirming feedback convinced me of the book's value, and since the original 2003 edition has long been out of print, I'm especially delighted that there's now an opportunity to present these thoughts to a new group of readers and aspiring astro-traders.

But in presenting this new edition of the book, I have not only tried to make it more useful. I also have had an opportunity to rectify an oversight. In doing so, I've felt that it's important to give credit where credit is due.

The fact is, many of the techniques and insights that make financial astrology such a powerful tool for market analysis and trading timing today came from the pivotal work of one individual who was first gaining his well-deserved reputation as a trading guru 100 years ago—W. D. Gann. And that's why I've changed the title of this newly revised and expanded edition to ***Gann Secrets Revealed***.

While I've personally never hesitated to give W. D. Gann the acknowledgment he deserves, in the past I have been a bit timid in openly associating my own work with Gann's methodologies. There's absolutely no question that W. D. Gann's approach to the markets set the standard for modern financial astrology, but unfortunately there have been some distortions and perversions of Gann's methodologies in recent years.

Indeed, during the past couple of decades we have seen the advent of an amazingly extensive cottage industry whose sole focus seems to be finding new ways of exploiting Gann's reputation and profiting from associations with his name, no matter how tenuous or improbable those associations may actually be.

The net result has been a lot of blatant rip-offs and misrepresentations, along with a few well-intentioned but essentially ineffective efforts at decoding parts of Gann's writings, presumably with the hope of discovering the One True Secret that will somehow unlock the mysteries of Gann's work and open the door to infinite wealth.

While such hopes are easy to sympathize with, I've been reluctant to risk being connected with an arena that is so susceptible to hype, distortion, and outright charlatanry.

In reality, W. D. Gann owed his success to hard work, persistence, and a remarkable ability to integrate his keen spiritual and metaphysical insights with his diligent observation of market patterns. He understood the Law of Vibration at many levels, from the patterns of his personal life to the movements of the markets, and it was that extraordinary first-hand understanding that opened up many potentially profitable opportunities for him throughout his life.

Unfortunately, there have been many traders, including many avid fans of Gann's work, who have entirely missed some of the key bits of knowledge that make his approach to the markets so powerful. Countless books and articles have been written on Gann's mathematical principles, on his charting techniques, and on his use of market geometry as an organizing force in his long-range analysis and predictive work.

While many of those efforts have been intelligently and passionately written, and while many of the principles they discuss were in fact used by Gann in his approach to the markets, most of the publications nevertheless fall short of the desired mark. The authors clearly have little or no real knowledge of astrology, or if they do know something about it they manage to conceal that fact very well. At any rate, astrology, if it is mentioned at all, is typically relegated to footnotes, or to implied assertions that Gann was some sort of "mad scientist" who succeeded in the markets through suspicious activities which were marred by his personal involvement in some very strange and disreputable areas, like astrology for example.

With *Gann Secrets Revealed* I'd like to do my part to help offset some of those misrepresentations. While this book is certainly not an effort to give a completely comprehensive explanation of W. D. Gann's astrology and the many ways that he used it in the markets, it does at least try to illuminate a few key astrological principles underlying some of his most significant work. I plan to explore more of Gann's contributions in one or more subsequent volumes in the future.

It's my sincere hope not only that you'll find the information in these pages useful and intellectually stimulating, but that you'll also become motivated to use these tools to sharpen your skills in astrologically-based market analysis, opening the door to more exciting and fulfilling experiences in the markets and to more profitable results from your trading. Along the way, if you're also inspired to explore the work of W. D. Gann in greater depth, I know you'll be much richer for the experience.

Tim Bost
Sarasota, Florida, USA
Mercury Direct Station
September 29, 2009

# W. D. Gann and Astrology

When you have access to something as powerful and as universally applicable as astrology, why not use it to get rich, enjoy your life more fully, and become more spiritually evolved, all at the same time?

That's exactly what the legendary trader and market forecaster W. D. Gann did in the last century.

Even then, the world of financial astrology—that remarkable realm where individuals use their own initiative to harness cosmic forces and control their own economic destiny—was populated with some truly extraordinary people. Gann was one of them.

William Delbert Gann was born on a cotton ranch near Lufkin, Texas, on June 6, 1878. When he was 24 years old, he began a career trading stocks and commodities.

W. D. Gann wasn't very successful when he first started trading in 1902. But he soon discovered the principles of financial astrology, and by the time he died in 1955, his estate was worth an estimated $5 million. (It's been said that during his lifetime he made over $55 million.)

He claimed that the secret to his success was that the stock market, like everything else in creation, responds to what he called the "Law of Vibration." Gann said that he learned about the Law of Vibration, a principle of absolute mathematical harmony, by reading the Bible from cover to cover. He then verified his discoveries with travels to England, where he studied rare manuscripts in the British Museum; to Egypt, where he pondered the mathematics of the pyramids; and to India, where he learned ancient vedic aphorisms about the divine correspondences behind market trends and fluctuations.

Although he wrote seven books and shared his ideas about the stock and commodities markets through advisory letters and trading courses, Gann's observations about the Law of Vibration never really gained many followers during his lifetime. He was, after all, a pioneering technical analyst in the days before technical market analysis was widely accepted—when it was even considered by some to be some sort of economic voodoo. And on top of that, he couched his explanations of the forces at work behind the markets in language replete with religious references and Masonic obscurities.

Nevertheless, the techniques that he developed were enough to help him start a trading account with $300 in 1908 and turn it into $25,000; and then open another account with only $130 and convert it to $12,000 in a single month!

The Law of Vibration also enabled W. D. Gann to forecast accurately the entire trading year of 1929 a full year in advance, including the historic stock market crash of 1929 and the beginning of the Great Depression that followed. His projections were so precise that he was able to predict not only the future direction for a particular stock or commodity, but also the exact date and price at which its trend would change.

"I believe in the stars," Gann wrote in 1927. "I believe in astrology, and I have figured out my destiny. The Bible makes it plain that the stars do rule." Astrological calculations were an integral part of his market forecasting work, and W. D. Gann was not only an accomplished astrologer himself, but also employed some of the most advanced astrologers of his day in preparing his analysis and forecasts for the markets.

Like many other noteworthy figures in the history of financial astrology, however, W. D. Gann didn't talk too much about astrology itself. In fact, in much of his writing he simply referred to astrological principles as "scientific" principles, at once simplifying and veiling the approach he was actually using. Over and over again, his mysterious methodology increased the size of his trading account, and brought substantial rewards to his clients and subscribers.

But in spite of the personal rewards he reaped from his trading and from marketing his study courses and advisory services, W. D. Gann apparently wasn't out to proselytize or to gain converts to financial astrology. He just preferred to get the benefits that this unique approach to the markets had to offer, so he could know ahead of time what the stock market was going to do, and go home with extra cash in his pocket at the end of each trading day.

It's exactly that potential that makes it worthwhile for every independent trader to learn and master the Gann Secrets that combine price and time with some unique astrological perspectives. Even so, it is important to remember that W. D. Gann had a unique understanding of what astrology is and how it works when he used it as a tool for enhancing the results he got from his trading.

That's part of what has been so challenging for Gann students who have tried to comprehend his use of astrology. Some have tried to ignore it altogether, while others have insisted that Gann's work actually had nothing to do with astrology at all.

Rather than get entangled in the arguments, our approach is simply to examine some of the ways that Gann took astrology beyond its conventional symbolic boundaries to develop methods that brought incredible accuracy to his forecasts and profits to his trading. But even as he did so, W. D. Gann never lost sight of the ways than genuine astrology can help individuals lead richer and more rewarding lives.

# FINDING THE PERSON IN FINANCIAL ASTROLOGY

W. D. Gann understood astrology. He knew that in its fullest flowering, financial astrology is a person-centered endeavor—it never ignores the real people whose lives are intimately linked to the money and the markets it studies.

Person-centered financial astrology helps enhance self-worth by providing a creative framework for managing financial change consciously and appropriately. It also empowers greater choice, creativity, and effectiveness by connecting the individual to financial opportunities in ways that acknowledge economic realities as latent sources of perpetual opportunity for mental, spiritual, and social growth, as well as for material well-being.

Person-centered financial astrology can help us step out of "victim mode" in our money matters as we progress into a broader and more comprehensive understanding of our latent potential for transforming ourselves, our expectations, and our sphere of influence.

In short, astrology in its finest expression simultaneously provides opportunities for fresh insight and deeper understanding while it empowers the kind of conscious growth that makes it possible for us to move past the limitations of who we have been and step forward into a fuller and more rewarding realization of who we are to become.

In or outside of the world of finance, astrology is a powerful tool for that kind of individual understanding and transformation primarily because it is a system of symbols.

As anyone who has had the opportunity to work personally with a skilled and compassionate professional astrologer fully understands, symbols are potent vehicles for moving rapidly past the boundaries and limitations of our habitual perceptions and our outmoded paradigms, giving us a particularly powerful way of enriching and expanding our experiences.

Thus it is that the planets, the horoscope houses, and the signs of the zodiac all connect us with a variegated world that is rich with meaning and nuance, opening up an incredible range of possibilities to the interpretive genius of the skilled astrologer. Under the guidance of a seasoned astrological professional, we can use the symbols of astrology to enhance our lives immeasurably, creating genuine wealth by expanding our mental, emotional, and spiritual potential along with our material well-being.

But even the most caring and competent astrologer, one who is attentive to human needs and who has gained considerable symbolic experience while perfecting the craft of integrative chart interpretation through extensive work with natal horoscopes and their more specialized derivatives, is faced with a unique challenge when it comes to using astrology as a forecasting tool for the equities and futures markets. Not all of the skills and experiences that an astrologer typically acquires may ultimately prove useful in developing financial forecasts. Indeed, some of them may actually get in the way.

The fact is, financial astrology is significantly different from other types of astrological practice. Person-centered financial astrology includes the all-important human perspective, but it rapidly becomes ineffective if it is allowed to default into uncritical psychobabble.

In the financial realm astrology has to do more than provide accurate and penetrating insights into the inner workings of individual personalities. It must also deliver useful, clear-cut information that can guide real-world market decisions. Financial astrology is more than just symbolism—while there is certainly an irrefutable correlation between celestial phenomena and significant actions in the equities markets, and while the correlation often provides glimpses of the inner workings of Natural Law, the nature of that correlation is not always a purely symbolic one.

In fact, would-be financial astrologers who try to dress market analysis in the garments of traditional astrological symbolism are often woefully wrong in their forecasts and interpretations. For example, a symbolically-oriented astrologer might reasonably expect the trading of shares of a company founded when the Sun was in Virgo to follow a distinctly different rhythm or pattern than the trading of shares of a company which began its operations with the Sun in Aries. Yet that is simply not always the case, and forecasts made on the basis of such naïve assumptions can be quite dangerous to the health of an investment portfolio!

We can of course speak of Taurean enterprises, of Uranian industries, of Mercurial advertising promotions, and of Capricornian managers. We can even erect natal horoscopes for companies and for their public stock offerings.

But when we use astrology to forecast price trends and reversals in equities markets we cannot depend on symbolic correspondences alone, at least not if we hope to come away from our market experiences with profits in our pockets. While the rich symbolism of astrology can be wonderfully useful in understanding ourselves and the psychological biases we bring to the markets as traders, when we consider the astrological dynamics of the equities markets themselves, our empirical experience and the demands of the market oblige us to consider celestial influences from a remarkably different, non-symbolic perspective. In short, we must be willing to move beyond symbolism in our financial astrology. That's what Gann did.

So what, then, actually constitutes an effective approach to the celestial dynamics involved in financial astrology? If we need to discover ways to de-emphasize traditional astrological symbolism as astro-traders or astrologers, what should we be using instead? Exactly what are the specific variables that we should consider if we are going to use an analysis of celestial phenomena to produce viable astrological forecasts for equities trends and prices?

In my view, based on my observations of Gann's work and the results he got, there are three major factors at the heart of effective astrological market analysis: the particular planets involved in a given astrological chart or transiting event, the type of planetary phenomena that those planets are participating in, and the specific vibratory resonances demonstrated by those celestial phenomena. All three of these major factors—planets, phenomena, and vibrations—certainly have rich and rewarding connections with esoteric traditions and the world of symbolism, but they do not necessarily derive their importance solely from that association. If we are at least temporarily willing to set aside the symbolic ramifications for the sake of more objective study, we are likely to discover that all three of these factors deserve our careful consideration as we strive to be successful in applying astrological tools to the equities and futures markets.

These three factors can give our market analysis meaning, vitality, and effectiveness. Once their impact has been taken into account—and only then—can some additional attention to traditional symbolism be safely added to our analysis. Symbolic insights can enormously enrich our understanding of our personal trading psychology, but they are best kept to a minimum when we examine the markets themselves. Like salt judiciously added to a pot of soup, symbolism can enhance our understanding of market dynamics, but it should never be served as a meal by itself, or stand alone as the basis for a forecast.

As Gann himself put it, "You cannot think about two things at the same time, nor can you do two things successfully at the same time." That's why it's best for us as astro-traders to set aside the symbolic implications of astrology long enough to experience some of the practical ways that the Law of Vibration really works.

# THE ROLE OF THE PLANETS

The first major factor in effective market analysis is the role of the planets themselves, specifically the transiting planets which add their energies to the environment of the markets by virtue of their current positions in the sky. Their importance is paramount. After all, the planets are the most active factors in astrology, and it is an analysis of action, particularly the up-and-down action of prices over time, that is the focus of our efforts to comprehend and anticipate the markets.

It's also worth noting that the planets are the factors in astrology that most fully embody the psychological dimensions of human behavior. Because the planets are connected with life's active psychological principles in general, and because equities markets are essentially nothing more than reflections of mass psychology as it fluctuates between the extremes of risk-adverse fear and overly-confident greed, we cannot afford to leave the transiting planets out of our forecasting considerations.

Our analysis can be considerably simplified, however, if we group the planets we are considering into two categories: the Lights of ancient and medieval astrology on the one hand, and all the other planets in our solar system on the other.

The Lights, i.e. the Sun and the Moon (which our colleagues peering through telescopes in astronomical observatories remind us are not really "planets" at all), have cycles that strongly correlate with seasonality in market trends and with annual cycles in the price fluctuations of some specific shares. They are also particularly useful in understanding and forecasting some short-term trading cycles.

The rhythmic interaction of the Sun and the Moon has served generation after generation as a durable and reliable clock in agricultural activities for countless thousands of years, and that same ancient archetype continues to make its influence felt in modern equities markets today. In fact, during the past few decades the lunar cycle and its relationship to the stock market has been extensively and systematically researched by Bill Meridian, Frank Guarino, Kathy Yuan, Lu Zheng, Qiaoqiao Zhu, David Hirshleifer, Tyler Shumway, and others.

Strictly speaking, the action of the lunar cycle is a series of planetary phenomena rather than an intrinsic property of the Sun and the Moon themselves, but it's nevertheless worth noting as a way of clarifying the distinction between considering the planets as symbolic forces and considering them more empirically as active agents of change.

The remaining major planets—Mercury, Venus, Mars, Jupiter, Saturn, Uranus, Neptune and Pluto—all have some influence on price movements in the markets, both individually and in various combinations with each other. There is, however, a direct correlation between the distance of a particular planet from the Sun and the overall strength and significance of its impact on the markets.

The basic principle here is that the further away a planet is from the Sun and the more slowly it moves through the zodiac, the stronger is its influence. Thus, while Mercury and Venus certainly make their impressions on market activity, it is the outer planets like Pluto, Neptune and Uranus that have the strongest effect.

Competent financial astrology takes these differences in relative distance and speed into consideration in trying to understand the potential impact of the planets, rather than simply focusing on the planets' symbolic distinctions as described by traditional astrology.

# PLANETARY PHENOMENA

The next major factor in assessing the influence of astrological dynamics in equities markets is the determination of the specific types of celestial phenomena that are under consideration.

One of the most basic of the celestial phenomena that impact the markets is the lunation cycle, the cycle of New Moons and Full Moons. As we've already noted, the correspondence of the lunation cycle to general price trends in the equities markets has been well documented by Frank Guarino, Ruth Miller, Bill Meridian and other more recent researchers. While the lunation cycle itself is obviously not the sole controller of market movements, it nonetheless should not be overlooked in our efforts to use astrological phenomena in forecasting market trends.

Eclipses represent special cases of the lunation cycle, with solar eclipses occurring only at New Moons and lunar eclipses coming only at Full Moons. Both solar eclipses and lunar eclipses can have a profound impact on the movement of equities prices.

Total solar eclipses are definitely the strongest market movers, followed in order of importance by annular solar eclipses, penumbral lunar eclipses, partial solar eclipses, partial lunar eclipses, and total lunar eclipses.

While the monthly lunation cycle sets up a background rhythm for market prices and while rudimentary interactions of the Sun and Moon with other planets rarely trigger shifts in the markets, the eclipses should never escape our attention as potential harbingers of significant trend changes.

Planetary stations, those moments in time when, from our earth-bound geocentric perspective, planets seem to halt in their orbital tracks and reverse direction, also have a considerable influence on market dynamics.

Experience has shown that Uranus stations are extremely strong market movers, even more powerful than lunar eclipses (but not as powerful as solar eclipses) in their ability to trigger trend changes.

Stations of Jupiter, Neptune, and Pluto are next in strength, followed by stations of Mars and Venus.

While Mercury stations seem to have a fairly weak effect on the markets, this planet's three-week periods of retrograde movement will sometimes correspond with short-term counter-trends in equities prices.

The next phenomena to note are the planetary conjunctions, especially the conjunctions of the outer planets. Because they occur relatively infrequently, outer planet conjunctions tend to have a more significant influence on the markets than conjunctions involving the Lights and the inner planets. In fact, outer planet conjunctions often show a stronger influence on market behavior than Mars or Venus stations.

Finally, we need to consider other planetary aspects. Of particular importance to the financial astrologer are the eighth-harmonic "hard" aspects—the square (90°), the opposition (180°), the semi-square (45°), and the sesquiquadrate (135°). These aspects do not have the impact that eclipses, planetary stations, and planetary conjunctions bring to bear on equities prices, but they do need to be taken into consideration when we prepare astrologically-based market forecasts or examine the trading potential of a specific stock or futures contract. As with planetary stations and conjunctions, the eighth-harmonic aspects of outer planets are typically more potent than aspects involving the inner planets.

# VIBRATORY RESONANCES

The third major factor that we need to consider in developing astrological market forecasts are the vibratory resonances generated by the planetary phenomena we've just described. These resonances exist because planetary phenomena do more than just indicate the potential for significant market activity—like a stone creating ripples on the surface of a pond, they also connect that potential with a specific set of locations in the circle of the zodiac.

Because of W. D. Gann's clear focus on the Law of Vibration as an indispensable component of his understanding of market dynamics, it's especially important for us as astro-traders to become intimately familiar with the various types of vibratory resonances, particularly if we hope to follow in Gann's footsteps. While this rudimentary discussion of vibratory resonance may not provide the definitive skeleton key that will unlock every door in the mysterious realm of Gann's more esoteric insights, it should at least help us focus on the kind of understanding that is crucial for effective astro-trading and that may also be vital for survival in a rapidly-changing market environment.

These vibratory resonances can be categorized and analyzed in three basic ways: resonance through location, resonance through activation by transit, and resonance through sympathetic dynamics. Each type of resonance has its own unique characteristics, but it is really the synergistic combination of all three types that makes them a major factor to consider in our market forecasts.

The first type of vibratory resonance, resonance through location, is simply a matter of paying attention to the zodiacal longitude of the particular planetary phenomenon we are considering.

For example, a solar eclipse is without a doubt an important factor that activates market action, but that eclipse does not take place in a vacuum, nor do all eclipses have the same effect on the markets.

Each solar or lunar eclipse, like every other planetary phenomenon, takes place at a specific location within the zodiac. Each location in zodiacal longitude carries its own vibratory essence, generates its own unique resonance, and creates its own distinctive potential for response in the equities markets.

In particular, this resonance of zodiacal position impacts price levels in actively traded markets that are not subject to extreme volatility. The vibratory resonance of zodiacal longitude also activates potential linkages between the transiting planetary phenomenon and key planets or other sensitive points in the natal horoscopes of individuals, businesses, stocks, or other entities.

The second type of vibratory resonance, resonance through activation by transit, builds on the conceptual foundation laid by resonance through location.

When additional transiting planets activate locations that have already become resonant by virtue of significant planetary phenomena, they expand and amplify the cumulative impact, and often provide a specific triggering effect that is reflected in market activity.

The basic notion here is that each eclipse or other planetary phenomenon will first "magnetize" or sensitize a particular degree of zodiacal longitude, creating a resonant field which can then be energized and set into motion by the transit of another planet across or in alignment to the same degree of zodiacal longitude. While various ancient and modern sources have expressed different opinions about just how long a sensitive degree can stay magnetized in this way, experience has shown that in many cases the residual effects can last for months or even years.

For example, a Neptune station at 10° Aquarius will sensitize that particular location in the zodiac, but an impact on the markets may not be felt until transiting Mars crosses over 10° Aquarius a week or so later, or perhaps when Venus reaches 10° Scorpio to form a square to the sensitive point that has previously been magnetized by the Neptune station.

The vibratory resonance through activation by transit thus has an important impact on the timing of market events—even though the initial planetary phenomenon sets up the resonant field to start with, it is actually the subsequent activation of that field by the additional transiting planet that typically coincides with a response in the markets.

The third type of vibratory resonance is resonance through sympathetic dynamics. Whenever a planetary phenomenon such as an eclipse or a planetary station occurs, it not only activates the particular degree of the zodiac at which it takes place— it also activates other points in the zodiac which share a sympathetic dynamic with the zodiacal location of the primary phenomenon.

In classical astrology, the antiscia, or solstice points, describe one particular type of resonant point that sets up a sympathetic dynamic with an activated point of zodiacal longitude. The antiscia involve reflections of planetary energies along the Cancer/Capricorn axis, which is the Cardinal sign alignment that acts as the meridian axis in the natural horoscope wheel.

Because the solar ingresses into Cancer and Capricorn each year mark the times of the Summer Solstice and the Winter Solstice, respectively, the antiscia have also come to be known as solstice points. Antiscia are thus positioned at distances from the Cancer/Capricorn axis that equal the distance of the initial zodiac point from that same axis, in a location that mirrors the position of the initial zodiac location.

In our contemporary astrological applications, however, we don't have to stop with the anticsia. Based on the notion that all Cardinal ingress points in the zodiac have special significance as potential mirrors of resonant planetary energy, we can turn to the Aries/Libra axis as a second important generator of sympathetic dynamics.

We can thus consider both the traditional solstice mirror points (the antiscia) and the equinoctial mirror points when we look for locations in zodiacal longitude that resonate with specific planetary phenomena through a sympathetic dynamic with primary vibratory points or resonant locations in the zodiac.

For example, an outer planet conjunction that takes place at 17° 19' Taurus will have two corresponding points that resonate through sympathetic dynamics: 12° 41' Leo (the antiscion) and 12° 41' Aquarius (the equinoctial mirror point).

In practical application, all three types of vibratory resonance— resonance through location, resonance through activation by transit, and resonance through sympathetic dynamics— work together seamlessly. By simultaneously considering all three types of vibratory resonance, we create a synergistic effect that significantly expands the horizons of our ability to forecast market trends.

# PUTTING IT ALL TOGETHER

To the novice, effective astrological analysis of potential trends and turning points in equities markets may seem like an overwhelming endeavor, even if we use Gann's techniques. If we follow the process systematically, however, we will discover that each component in the analysis complements and enhances all of the others.

Seen in its entirety, our preliminary procedure for astrological market analysis includes the following steps:

First, we determine which planet or planets are most strongly involved as current factors in the market environment, or are most likely to make their influence felt in the future as that market environment evolves.

Second, we note which specific planetary phenomena are in effect— are we looking at eclipses, at planetary stations, or at some other phenomenon?

Third, we note which degree of the zodiac is activated by each specific phenomenon, by virtue of vibratory resonance through the zodiacal longitude of the phenomenon.

Fourth, we turn to the ephemeris and list the dates of upcoming transits to the resonant point in the zodiac, as well as to the corresponding fourth-harmonic points (the squares and the opposition point).

Fifth, we calculate the zodiacal locations of the cardinal mirrors—the antiscia and the equinoctial mirror points that correspond with the resonant location of the planetary phenomenon.

# CALCULATING EQUINOCTIAL MIRROR POINTS

Equinoctial mirrored zodiacal positions, the sympathetic dynamic points which are generated by the Aries/Libra axis in the natural horoscope wheel, can be precisely determined by subtracting the degree positions within a particular zodiac sign from the constant arc of 30°, then adding the mirrored sign.

Use the following list to determine quickly which zodiac sign mirrors which other sign:

Aries mirrors into Pisces

Libra mirrors into Virgo


Taurus mirrors into Aquarius

Scorpio mirrors into Leo


Gemini mirrors into Capricorn

Sagittarius mirrors into Cancer


Cancer mirrors into Sagittarius

Capricorn mirrors into Gemini


Leo mirrors into Scorpio

Aquarius mirrors into Taurus


Virgo mirrors into Libra

Pisces mirrors into Aries


If we let X represent the degree position within the original sign and A represent the original sign itself; and if we let Y represent the degree position within the mirrored sign and M represent the equinoctial mirrored sign, we can say that:

$$360 - (A + 30) = M$$

and

$$30 - X = Y$$

Thus, with 20° 15' Cancer we can say that $X = 20.25$ and $A = 90$, so the equinoctial mirrored degree is:

$$30 - X = Y$$
$$30 - 20.25 = Y$$
$$9.75 = Y$$

$$360 - (A + 30) = M$$
$$360 - (90 + 30) = M$$
$$360 - 120 = M$$
$$240 = M$$

$Y + M = 9.75 + 240 = 249.75$ or 9° 45' Sagittarius.

In another example, if we wish to find the equinoctial mirrored point for 12° 39' Taurus we can say that X = 12.65 and A = 30, so the equinoctial mirrored degree is:

$$30 - X = Y$$
$$30 - 12.65 = Y$$
$$17.35 = Y$$

$$360 - (A + 30) = M$$
$$360 - (30 + 30) = M$$
$$360 - 60 = M$$
$$300 = M$$

Y + M = 17.35 + 300 = 317.35 or 17° 21' Aquarius.

# CALCULATING ANTISCIA

The antiscia can be calculated in a similar fashion, with the mirroring factor aligning along the Cancer/Capricorn axis instead of along the Aries/Libra axis. Thus, in determining antiscia, we simply subtract the degree position within a zodiac sign from the constant arc of 30°, and then add the appropriate mirrored sign:

> Aries mirrors into Virgo
> Libra mirrors into Pisces
>
> Taurus mirrors into Leo
> Scorpio mirrors into Aquarius

Gemini mirrors into Cancer

Sagittarius mirrors into Capricorn

Cancer mirrors into Gemini

Capricorn mirrors into Sagittarius

Leo mirrors into Taurus

Aquarius mirrors into Scorpio

Virgo mirrors into Aries

Pisces mirrors into Libra

It's worth noting that when we calculate equinoctial mirror points, they will always be in opposition to (180° away from) the corresponding antiscia. We can thus speed up the calculation process by determining the equinoctial mirror points first, and then simply changing the zodiacal signs to their polar opposites to derive the corresponding antiscia.

# A MARKET MYSTERY

Once these five steps have been completed, we have the key information at hand that will ultimately allow us to draw conclusions about anticipated trends in the equities markets. But we are still faced with one of the mysteries of market analysis—even if we can accurately forecast an overall market trend, that trend may or may not apply to a particular individual stock.

Indeed, the application of astrology to the financial markets is particularly challenging because stock market astrology is simultaneously the study of cosmically influenced movements of mass psychology that impact markets as a whole, and the study of thousands of individual business entities. These business entities all have their own unique natal characteristics, and all of them that are publicly traded also have their corresponding equities (which display particular characteristics of their own, as distinguished from the companies themselves) and, in some cases, derivative instruments like puts and calls as well.

One of the axioms of the stock market is that a rising tide floats all boats—an overall trend in the market typically dictates the price trend for more than 75% of the stocks being traded. But what about the exceptions, the stocks that don't behave like the rest of the market? How do we determine whether a particular equity will follow the trend of the broader market or whether it will march to the beat of a different drummer?

One potential answer lies in the individual horoscopes associated with the companies we are examining. The horoscope for the company's founding or incorporation, along with its progressed astrological derivatives and current transits, will often yield important insights that may reasonably lead us to predict circumstances that do not necessarily match the general expectations for the market.

Even more useful is the horoscope for the first trade of the company's stock. While incorporation horoscopes are representations of companies themselves, First-Trade horoscopes are representations of the actual equities, the shares of the company's stock that are traded in a bourse or stock exchange.

First-Trade charts, originally used by George Bayer and subsequently given substantial refinement as a trading tool by Bill Meridian, are calculated for the time at which the first shares of the company's stock are available to change hands on a public exchange. Note that this is typically different than the Initial Public Offering (IPO) date for a publicly traded company, since IPOs are usually limited to transactions by company insiders, offering underwriters, and institutional investors who have made advance commitments to purchasing specific blocks of the new shares. The First-Trade date follows the IPO; it marks the time that members of the general public are first able to buy and sell shares of the stock on the open market once they have been listed on an exchange.

The angles and key planets in a First-Trade horoscope are sensitive points that typically respond to planetary transits with corresponding movements or with trend changes in share prices.

But for the purpose of developing accurate market forecasts, the most important thing to note about First-Trade horoscopes is that they give us a way of looking at various equities as unique entities, each with its own individual potential for responding to the cosmic factors that move markets.

The planetary phenomena and vibratory resonances that impact market behavior in general ways will thus manifest themselves in remarkably different specific ways, depending upon the different factors at work in various First-Trade horoscopes.

For example, a Uranus retrograde station will typically correspond with a broad-based trend change in stock market prices, but it will make its influence felt much more noticeably upon the share prices of stocks whose First-Trade Ascendants are conjunct the zodiacal longitude of the Uranus station.

In practical application, the most effective method of identifying the companies whose stocks will show the strongest response to an upcoming market-moving planetary phenomenon is to begin by determining the zodiacal positions of the phenomenon and its concomitant antiscia and equinoctial mirror points. Then, using these specific zodiacal positions as the search criteria, the financial astrologer can scan a computerized database or simply review a printed listing of key points in First-Trade horoscopes to determine which specific equities will be most closely impacted by the particular planetary phenomenon that's coming up.

Ultimately, though, the real secret to using these planetary tools derived from W. D. Gann's work boils down to one thing—experience.

As Gann students, astro-traders, or financial astrologers, we all sooner or later discover that there is no substitute for hard work. If we persist in our application of Gann-inspired astrological principles and in our personal observations of real-world market behavior, we eventually gain enough personal experience with the astrological dimensions of the markets to see connections and opportunities that were completely invisible to our eyes before—and that's when we can begin to trade more profitably.

# POWER NUMBERS

It's worth noting that there is another method of correlating planetary phenomena to individual equities, one which does not use the First-Trade or incorporation horoscopes. This method is particularly useful when an exact First-Trade horoscope is not available for one reason or another, but it can also provide helpful corroboration of the conclusions that we might reach through First-Trade horoscope analysis. It is the method that uses "Power Numbers" to identify particular equities as candidates for activation by upcoming planetary phenomena.

The "Power Number" principle is a very simple one. Its basic premise is that sensitive spots in the zodiac, as determined by eclipses or other planetary phenomena (or by key points in a natal or corporate horoscope), can all be translated into specific "Power Numbers." These Power Numbers are particular numerical values which correspond with lively vibratory focal points and which can be used for price analysis, for determining support and resistance zones for equities and futures, or for other purposes.

There are just four basic guidelines to follow in converting positions in zodiacal longitude to Power Numbers: sign/degree equivalence, decimalization, movement of the decimal point, and amplification by circular increments. When these four guidelines are all taken into consideration together, it becomes possible to derive a variety of Power Numbers from an astrological phenomenon at any planetary position, based solely on the phenomenon's location in zodiacal longitude.

The first consideration is sign/degree equivalence. Because the circle of the zodiac is 360° and because each zodiac sign is exactly 30° wide, there is a direct numerical correspondence between each position in a sign and a specific degree number. The starting degree numbers for each sign of the zodiac are:

Aries – 0

Taurus – 30

Gemini – 60

Cancer – 90

Leo – 120

Virgo – 150

Libra – 180

Scorpio – 210

Sagittarius – 240

Capricorn – 270

Aquarius – 300

Pisces – 330

Each position in a sign can thus be converted to a rudimentary Power Number simply by adding the degree positions within the sign to the starting degree position of that particular zodiac sign. Thus:

12° Aries becomes 12

(12 + 0 = 12)

19° Cancer becomes 109

(19 + 90 = 109)

22° Virgo becomes 172

(22 + 150 = 172)

7° Aquarius becomes 307

(7 + 300 = 307)

and so on.

The second consideration in deriving Power Numbers is the decimalization of minutes and seconds. Fractional portions of degrees in zodiacal longitude, traditionally represented as minutes and seconds, can be used to extend the Power Number concept by converting the fractions to decimal notation, in combination with the principle of sign/degree equivalence. Thus:

11°30' Taurus becomes 41.5

(11°30' = 11.5 + 30 = 41.5)

22°18' Leo becomes 142.3

29°13'14" Scorpio becomes 239.22

2°10'58" Capricorn becomes 272.18 and so on.

The third consideration is the movement of the decimal point. Power Numbers can also be modified by simple movement of the decimal point, especially when fractional values are present. Thus:

27°41'03" Libra = 207.684 = 20.7684 = 2076.84

or

13° Aquarius = 313 = 3.13 = 31.3 = 3130

The final consideration in deriving Power Numbers is amplification by circular increments. Simply stated, any Power Number can be amplified by adding 360 or a multiple of 360 to it, based on the notion (as developed by W.D. Gann, who also used a Wheel of 24) that revolutions around a 360° circle can be represented as concentric wheels, with each position on an inner wheel corresponding to a position on the next-outermost wheel that is 360° higher than the original inner wheel position. A Power Number can thus be amplified by 360° circular increments:

$$22° \text{ Leo} \quad = 142$$
$$= (142 + 360) = 502$$
$$= (142 + 360 + 360) = 862$$

*or*

$$17° \ 12' \text{ Taurus} = 47.2$$
$$= (47.2 + 360) = 407.2$$
$$= (47.2 + 360 + 360) = 767.2$$

Once a series of Power Numbers has been derived from the zodiacal longitude of a planetary phenomenon and its concomitant antiscion and equinoctial mirror point, it's a very simple matter to convert the Power Numbers to monetary equivalents, corresponding to the current prices of specific equities. Thus:

$$9° \; 15' \; \text{Virgo} = 159.25 = \$159.25 = \$15.93$$

and

$$(159.25 + 360) = 519.25 = \$51.93$$

with the antiscion:

$$20° \; 45' \; \text{Aries} = 20.75 = \$20.75 = (20.75 + 360) = 380.75 =$$
$$\$38.08$$

and the equinoctial mirror point:

$$20° \; 45' \; \text{Libra} = 200.75 = \$200.08 =$$
$$(200.75 + 360) = \$56.08$$

An eclipse or a planetary station at 9° 15' Virgo could thus be expected to resonate in a particularly strong way with stocks priced at $15.93, $20.08, $20.75, $38.08, $51.93, $56.08, $159.25, and $200.75.

The advantage that this method provides is an obvious one—instead of searching a database of First-Trade horoscopes, an astro-trader trying to fine-tune a market forecast can derive Power Numbers, determine their price equivalents, and then search for corresponding equity prices in published stock market tables or online databases.

Of course, in order to refine this method, it is best to follow up predictive hypotheses with empirical observation—if a particular stock closes at a Power Number price level when transiting Mars conjoins the eclipse point two weeks later, the observant financial astrologer can feel much more confident in forecasting another return to the same price level for the stock when the next transit to the eclipse point comes up in the ephemeris!

Because it is such an exacting endeavor, astrological forecasting of equities markets requires clarity, focus, and persistence from the skilled astro-trader or financial astrologer. As astro-traders, we will not only discover that a disciplined approach to our trading and analysis will bring us more consistent results and enhanced profits, even though we will inevitably experience losses from time to time—we will more clearly understand what W. D. Gann meant when he said that "Misfortunes and adversities often prove a blessing in disguise. We must learn by past mistakes and not repeat them in the future." Along the way, we are also likely to be amazed at the extra power and money-making potential that the astrological edge brings to our encounters with the markets.

From the point of view of financial astrologers there's a big payoff as well. If the astrologer rigorously follows all of the necessary steps for precise astrological market analysis, intuitive breakthroughs will spontaneously interject themselves into the analytical process. Increasing experience brings increasing insight. And when the financial astrologer becomes completely comfortable with a disciplined approach to stock market astrology, there will also be room for the reintroduction of traditional astrological symbolism—in moderate amounts, of course.

Even more important, the astrologer who masters disciplined market analysis can offer something truly significant to the client seeking astrological guidance in investments—a caring approach that honors the individual and centers the counseling on pragmatic, person-centered concerns. But that close and creative personal connection with the client can only take place when the astrologer, following in the footsteps of W. D. Gann, is sublimely confident in the reliability of the techniques being used for analysis and forecasting.

Needless to say, the client who works with such an astrologer can enjoy profound personal enrichment and real strategic security in confronting life's changes and challenges. In the process, the astrologer can gain much personal and professional validation from the connection, all the while resting certain in the knowledge that the broad equities markets—and even the fortunes to be found in individual stocks—will ultimately yield all their secrets to the tools and techniques pioneered by W. D. Gann in the development of modern financial astrology.

# Suggested Reading and Additional Resources

- Bayer, George: *Time Factors in the Stock Market*, 1937.

- Bayer, George: *Turning Four Hundred Years of Astrology to Practical Use and Other Matters*, 1943.

- Bost, Tim: *Basic Stock Market Astrology Home Study Course*, Harmonic Research Associates, 2004.

- Carolan, Christopher: *The Spiral Calendar and Its Effect on Financial Markets and Human Events*, New Classics Library, 1992.

- Droke, Clif: *Gann Simplified*, Marketplace Books, 2001.

- Farrell, Paul B.: *Think Astrology and Grow Rich*, Money Astrology Research Institute, 1993.

- Gann, W. D.: *How to Make Profits in Commodities*, Library of Gann Publishing Co. Inc., 1942.

- Gann, W. D.: *The Magic Word*, 1950.

- Gann, W. D.: *The Tunnel Thru The Air or Lookng Back from 1940*, Lambert-Gann Publishing Company, 1927.

- Gann, W. D.: *Truth of the Stock Tape*, Financial Guardian Publishing Co., 1923.

- Jensen, Luther J.: ***Astro-Cycles and Speculative Markets***, Lambert-Gann Publishing Company, 1961.

- Krausz, Robert: ***A W. D. Gann Treasure Discovered: Simple Trading Plans for Stocks & Commodities***, Geometric Traders Institute, Inc.

- Long, Jeanne: ***Basic Astrotech: A New Technique for Trading Commodities Using Geocosmic Energy Fields with Technical Analysis***, PAS Astro-Soft, Inc., 1989.

- Long, Jeanne: ***Universal Clock: Forecasting Time and Price in the Footsteps of W. D. Gann, Book 1***, PAS Astro-Soft, Inc., 1993.

- Meridian, Bill: ***Planetary Stock Trading III***, Cycles Research Publications, 2002.

- Merriman, Raymond: ***The Ultimate Book on Stock Market Timing: Geocosmic Correlations to Trading Cycles***, MMA/Seek-It Publications, 2001.

- Mikula, Patrick B.: **_Gann's Scientific Methods Unveiled Volume 1_**, Patrick Mikula Publishing and Trading, 1995.

- Mikula, Patrick B.: **_Gann's Scientific Methods Unveiled Volume 2_**, Vibration Research Institute, 1996.

- Pesavento, Larry: **_Planetary Harmonics of Speculative Markets_**, Astro-Cyles, 1990.

- Renz, Curt: **_The Investor's Guide to Technical Analysis_**, McGraw-Hill, 2004.

- Rieder, Thomas: **_Sun Spots, Stars, and the Stock Market_**, Pagurian Press, 1979.

- Weingarten, Henry: **_Investing by the Stars_**, McGaw-Hill, 1996.

- www.FinancialCyclesWeekly.com

- www.GalacticInvestor.com

- www.GannPlan.com

# ABOUT THE AUTHOR

Tim Bost's work as a forecaster and consultant is not only informed by more than 40 years of intensive astrological study and experience; Tim's clients and readers benefit as well from his varied background in marketing, education, religion, business management, healing, and the arts. Since 1988, Tim has also gained international recognition as one of the world's leading authorities on the correlation between planetary patterns and price movements in the equities markets.

It was in 1988 that Tim Bost began publishing his market newsletter, **Financial Cycles Weekly**, a widely-read publication that has been cited in *Barron's*, the *Chicago Tribune*, *Bridge News*, and a variety of other national and regional business publications. In addition to publishing **Financial Cycles Weekly**, Tim conducts research into astrologically-based trading systems and counsels individual and corporate clients throughout the world. He has written regular astrology columns for a variety of publications including *Natural Awakenings*, the *Independent Observer*, the *Sarasota Herald-Tribune*, and *InParadise* magazine. He has also appeared as a regular guest commentator on Michael Yorba's *Commodity Classics* television program.

In 1993 Tim contributed a chapter to the Llewellyn Publications anthology, **How To Manage The Astrology of Crisis.** Noel Tyl, the anthology's editor and one of the world's most widely respected astrologers, said that Tim's contribution—on using astrology as a tool for managing financial crisis—was "one of the handful of truly superb articles I have ever read in astrology." Tim's writings have also been translated into Russian for inclusion in an advanced textbook on financial astrology.

During his years as a professional astrologer and market analyst Tim Bost has gained a reputation for accurate and insightful prognostication. In the summer of 2000, for example, Tim published a forecast that correctly predicted the exact date in September of that year which would mark the end of a history-making rally in stocks and the beginning of the bear market that brought the bursting of the dot-com bubble. His stunningly accurate forecast merited a headline in *Barron's* and brought him much favorable attention in the financial world.

Tim Bost has been a regular contributor to *A Traders Astrological Almanac* and a featured speaker at many financial conferences and astrology conventions. He holds professional memberships and the highest levels of certification from the American Federation of Astrologers, the National Council on Geocosmic Research, and the International Society for Astrological Research, and is active in AFAN, the International Society for Business Astrology, and other professional organizations.

A native of North Carolina, Tim currently lives in Sarasota, Florida.

*For More Information:*
www.FinancialCyclesWeekly.com
www.BasicMarketCourse.com
www.GannPlan.com
www.TimBost.com

For a free subscription to Tim Bost's exclusive Astro-Traders' Tip of the Week email service, go to http://www.FinancialCyclesWeekly.com and sign up today!

www.ingramcontent.com/pod-product-compliance
Lightning Source LLC
Chambersburg PA
CBHW020315220326
41598CB00017BA/1560